A

CW00403903

TO
BRITISH

A POCKET GUIDE TO TRANSLATING ENGLISH TO ENGLISH

So you don't look stupid
when trying to understand
American English words

PREFACE

Most Brits travelling to America don't expect there to be a language barrier but there are more differences in American vs British words than you think. This mini illustrated 'dictionary' is here to rescue you.

CHEERS!

ALLOWANCE

POCKET MONEY

ANTENNA

AERIAL

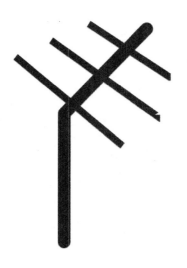

APARTMENT

FLAT

ATTORNEY

SOLICITOR

BAKED POTATO

JACKET POTATO

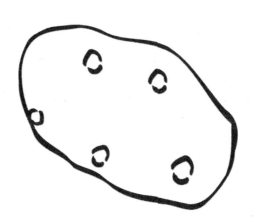

BABY BUGGY

PRAM

BACK UP

REVERSE

BALL POINT PEN

BIRO

BAND-AID

PLASTER

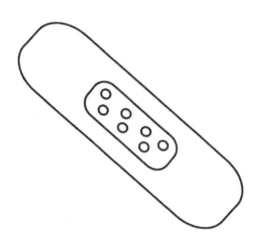

BAR

PUB

CHECK

BILL

CAB

TAXI

CAN

TIN

CANDY

SWEETS

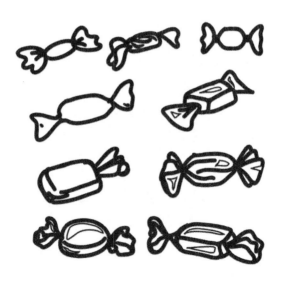

CELLPHONE

MOBILE

CILANTRO

CORIANDER

CLOTHES PIN

CLOTHES PEG

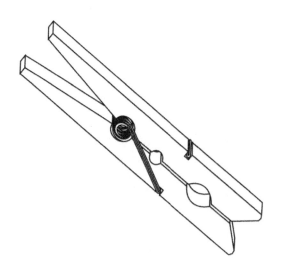

COLLECT CALL

REVERSE CHARGE

COOKIE

BISCUIT

COSTUME

FANCY DRESS

COTTON
CANDY

CANDY FLOSS

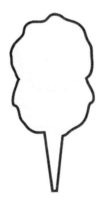

COUNTER - CLOCKWISE

ANTI-CLOCKWISE

CRAZY

MAD

CRIB

COT

DESSERT

PUDDING

DETOUR

DIVERSION

DIAPER

NAPPY

DISH TOWEL

TEA TOWEL

DIVIDED HIGHWAY

DUAL CARRIAGEWAY

DRIVER LICENSE

DRIVING LICENCE

EGGPLANT

AUBERGINE

ELEVATOR

LIFT

ERASER

RUBBER

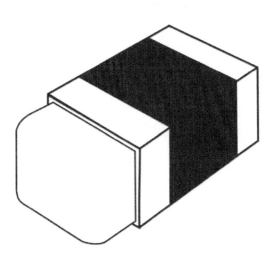

FALL

AUTUMN

FANNY

BUM

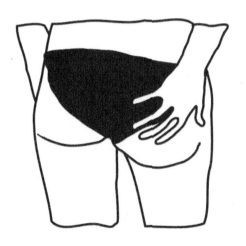

FAUCET

TAP

FLASHLIGHT

TORCH

FOOTBALL

AMERICAN FOOTBALL

FREEWAY

MOTORWAY

FRIES

CHIPS

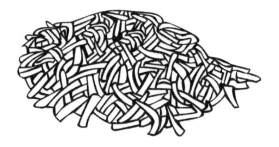

GARBAGE CAN

RUBBISH BIN

GARBAGE COLLECTOR

DUSTMAN

GAS

PETROL

GAS PEDAL

ACCELERATOR

GEAR SHIFT

GEAR STICK

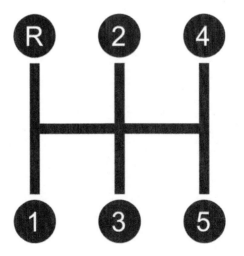

GERMAN SHEPHERD

ALSATIAN

HAMBURGER BUN

BAP

HIGHWAY

MAIN ROAD

HOOD

BONNET

INTERSECTION

CROSSROAD

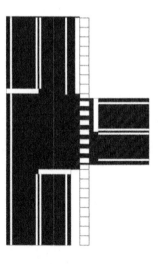

JANITOR

CARETAKER

LADYBUG

LADYBIRD

LINE

QUEUE

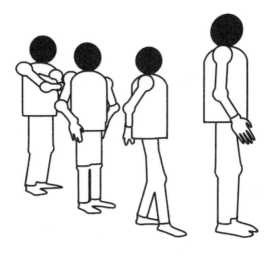

MAIL

POST

MAILBOX

POSTBOX

MAILMAN

POSTMAN

MATH

MATHS

MOTORCYCLE

MOTORBIKE

MOVIE

FILM

OATMEAL

PORRIDGE

ONE-WAY TICKET

SINGLE TICKET

PACIFIER

DUMMY

PANTS

TROUSERS

PERIOD

FULL STOP

●

PARENTHESES

BRACKETS

(   )

PARKING LOT

CAR PARK

PET PEEVE

PET HATE

PHARMACY

CHEMIST

POPSICLE

ICE LOLLY

POTATO CHIPS

CRISPS

PRESERVE

JAM

PRINCIPAL

HEAD TEACHER

PRIVATE
SCHOOL

PUBLIC SCHOOL

RAILROAD

RAILWAY

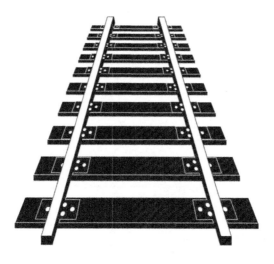

REALTOR

ESTATE AGENT

RECESS

BREAK

RESUME

CV

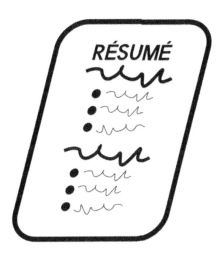

REST ROOM

TOILET

ROUND TRIP

RETURN

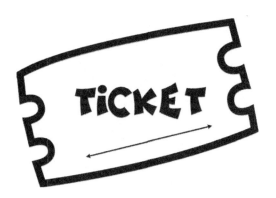

SCHEDULE

TIMETABLE

SEDAN

SALOON

SIDEWALK

PAVEMENT

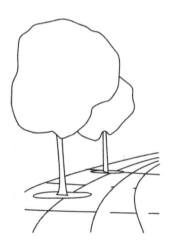

SLINGSHOT

CATAPULT

SNEAKERS

TRAINERS

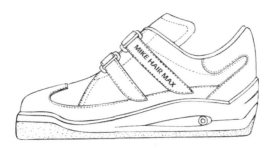

SOCCER

FOOTBALL

STORE

SHOP

STOVE

COOKER

SUBWAY

UNDERGROUND

SWEATER

JUMPER

TEXAS GATE

CATTLE GRID

TIRE

TYRE

THUMBTACK

DRAWING PIN

TIC TAC TOE

NAUGHT AND CROSSES

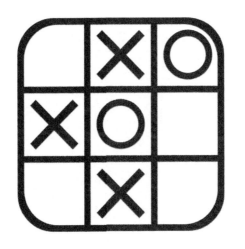

TRASH CAN

DUSTBIN

TRUCK

LORRY

TRUNK

BOOT

TWO WEEKS

FORTNIGHT

UNDERWEAR

PANTS

VACATION

HOLIDAY

VACUUM CLEANER

HOOVER

VEST

WAISTCOAT

WINDSHIELD

WINDSCREEN

WRENCH

SPANNER

YARD SALE

JUMBLE SALE

ZIP CODE

POSTCODE

ZIPPER

ZIP

ZUCCHINI

COURGETTE